Georgette the Bear

Dolly Johnson

Georgette the Bear

Dolly Johnson

First Printing

10 9 8 7 6 5 4 3 2 1

ISBN 978-1-936711-56-7

Railroad Street Press
394 Railroad Street., Suite 2
St. Johnsbury, Vermont 05819

This is a true story about a little cub that came to us in 2010, and we watched her grow from a cub to a mother of her own. She came around for five years. I hope you enjoy the story as much as we did watching her.

Georgette the Bear

Georgette looked down from the tree her Mother had sent her up and wondered where her Mother could have gone. It had been a long time and she hadn't come back yet.

"I have to get something to eat. I'm awful hungry." I wonder what the creature is putting out. He seemed to be real friendly and acted like he wanted to help. She decided to check it out. She found seed on the ground and took a bit. "Yuk! This is awful." And she spit it out. She wandered a little further down the hill and snipped off a plant that didn't taste too bad. She sat and ate a little of these plant heads. At least it helped a little.

She started exploring the bank and was discovering a lot of fun things to play with. First, she found a big metal toolbox and wondered what on earth it was.

Georgette was having so much fun checking out things that she was unaware that her picture was being taken every time she found a new toy to explore. She knew these people were good people and wanted to help her, not hurt her, so she wasn't afraid anymore.

"This is fun, and I'm staying here where I know I am safe." Georgette was happy here and felt safe. The man talked to her and Georgette would walk toward him but as soon as she got close the man would say something and she knew she was close enough so she backed off.

5-9-11

Georgette knew she needed to find a winter home where it would be warm. She found a hollow tree not far from the man's house. It was out of the wind and she felt safe here. She crawled in and soon was snuggled in for the winter.

She woke once to find the man and another person looking at her, but she wasn't afraid and fell back to sleep.

She soon had the urge to come out and see what was going on around her. She wandered down the hill and onto the man's lawn checking out things to eat on the way. She took a drink out of the waterfall and walked on.

If only she could find something to eat. Georgette knew she needed to find something soon. She was losing all her fur. She watched as the man put out food in a pan for another furry creature. Should she be afraid of this? She didn't think so as she watched the man and creature go inside. She wandered down to check whatever this was in the pan. She took a bite and another. "Hmm, this is good. She ate until it was all gone and tipped the pan over and started playing with it. Soon the man came back outside and refilled the pan.

She watched as he did this and thought so if I turn the pan over, he'll bring more food. She was all for that. She liked it here and decided to stay for another year.

Georgette had a whole yard she played in. She often stopped to get a drink and checked out the pretty flowers in the flower beds. She tried eating one of the flowers but the lady yelled out of the window at her. "Oh oh, I don't think I should have done that." She backed away from the flowers as she didn't want to make the lady angry. Her fur was growing back and she knew it was because of the help she received from these nice people.

If was time for her to find a winter home again. She had explored places away from her home here and found another hollow tree to stay for this winter. It was that time again.

Georgette knew she'd be back in the spring. She was feeling very healthy and this was her home.

When Georgette woke up in the spring, she had to check on her home place to be sure the homeowners were okay.

She stopped to get a drink and see what else was new, often watching from the hill while the man mowed the grass.

She felt good now and had found food on her own. She was three years old and getting big. She roamed the neighborhood checking on other places but she always came back here where she knew she was safe.

When Georgette woke up the following spring she had two little cubs. She knew they would be safe at the man's home but she wanted to check it out first. She first stopped to get a drink. She saw the man watching her and knew everything was okay. They acted real glad to see her and she was glad to see them.

She called her cubs and they came running down the hill. She wasn't worried as she knew these people and they would be glad to see her babies.

Georgette was proud of her babies and she taught them to drink from the waterfalls and that the flower beds were a no, no.

Every third day or so she'd take her babies and roam the neighborhood. She always came back to the man's house. This is where she called home. Her babies were growing and learning new things on their own. She kept a watchful eye on them to be sure they stayed out of trouble.

She found a safe place to winter her babies and then in the spring she was back with her babies. The babies were still small but Georgette found a new beau and even a third one tried to butt in. She chased her babies up a tree to keep them safe.

Her cubs would be on their own now. She had done her job. It was time to move on.

Georgette the Bear

This is the story of a little bear cub that came to us in the 2010.

We were outside one day and saw a small bear cub in a tree near our front lawn. We waited to see if the Mother would show up, but she never did. My husband started talking to the cub and eventually it came down the tree. It seemed very uncertain on what to do next. It looked awfully small to be out on her own, but it was bear season so we thought the Mother might have been shot. She would not have gone off and left the cub without some reason.

My husband had just filled the bird feeders and wondered if the cub would try to get at the seeds.

We thought the cub was a boy so we called him Georgie.

He started exploring on the bank around the yard. He even started coming within a few feet of my husband. He wasn't afraid and when my husband talked to him and said, "You're so close Georgie." The bear would stop and back off, almost as if he understood.

Georgie would play and explore and one day he pulled a PVC pipe off the bank and started playing and rolling around on the lawn with it. That was when we realized Georgie was a she. So we changed her name to Georgette.

Every day we watched her play and roll around. She was having so much fun. We were also having fun watching her. She would sit on the bank and watch us mow the lawn. We had a waterfall on the bank and she would occasionally get in the tub.

The second year she came back on April 17th, 2011. My husband and daughter had found the tree she hibernated in the week before and checked on her. She looked at them and went back to sleep. The following week when she came out she looked very haggard.

My husband was very concerned about her as she wasn't eating anything as far as he could tell. She looked awful skinny and was losing all her hair. He finally set a dish of dog food out in the yard as we had a new puppy. We walked back inside and soon she was testing the pan of dog food. She ate it all and started playing with the dish.

Her hair started growing back and she became a healthy looking cub again. She was getting braver and wandered around the neighborhood. She came around every third day or so checking on us.

She was so much fun to watch and she never seemed to be bothered by us as we took many pictures of her.

September 19, 2011 was the last time we saw Georgette for that year.

April 7, 2012. We saw a bear on the bank. We watched her to see what she would do. Georgette always had a favorite place where she would sit and watch us so we waited to see if this bear was our Georgette.

Sure enough, it wasn't long before she came down and sat in her favorite place. It was Georgette.

My husband talked to her and she watched him for a while before she started down to meet him.

"That's close enough Georgette." He would say and she stopped and watched him.

It's nice to know that in all the years she came around she never bothered our bird feeders.

She would wander down to where the dog dish was and if it was empty, she'd turn it upside down as if to say, "It's empty can't you see?"

We took so many pictures of her just playing with the empty pan. After a while she'd wander off and find something else to eat or play with. Sometimes she'd just sit and watch us go about our business.

Every day Georgette would come by and sit and watch us. It was almost as if she was checking to see if we were okay.

She would drink from the waterfall we had on the bank. And if we were sitting outside she'd come down to see us, but always stayed her distance, never getting dangerously close.

She was just so much fun to watch, but we knew this was a wild bear, and we were always aware of this fact.

The last of us seeing her for 2012 was October 20th. She was getting big by then.

It was May 23, 2013, when Georgette came around again and she had two little baby cubs with her. We knew it was her by the way she acted and it was almost as if she knew we would be okay with her babies.

We had been so worried about her all spring, wondering if she had made it through another winter.

2013 brought many pictures and many memories of Georgette and her babies. It was fun to watch them play as had been when Georgette was little.

Now we had three bears to watch play and they would drink from the tub where the waterfall was.

September 13, 2013 was the last time we saw Georgette and her cubs that year.

April 29, 2014, Georgette and her cubs were back.

We were so glad to see them. This would make the 5th year for these visits. Georgette was still coming down to visit us now and then. The cubs would come half way, but would stop and watch us. I think they might have been taught to be cautious about things, at least I'm hoping they were.

About the middle of summer Georgette started chasing her cubs away and there were two male bears hanging around so we knew Georgette was in heat again.

For two months Georgette would come down and another bear right behind her. Her cubs were still around, but Georgette would chase them up a tree. We thought maybe it was to keep them safe from the male bear.

June of 2014 was our last sighting of Georgette.

We never saw her again. The cubs drifted away and we didn't see them either.

I hate to think anything bad happened to Georgette, but know all things must come to an end at some point. We had fun watching them grow and watched Georgette grow from a cub to a Mother with many pictures along the way.

My only hope is that Georgette and her cubs are enjoying life in the wild like it was always meant to be.

www.ingramcontent.com/pod-product-compliance
Lightning Source LLC
Chambersburg PA
CBHW060840270326
41933CB00002B/153